T0197223

Module 2
Mary Magdalen's Current Sacred Mission

K I M C I N T I O

BALBOA.PRESS
A DIVISION OF HAY HOUSE

Balboa Press books may be ordered through booksellers or by contacting:

Balboa Press
A Division of Hay House
1663 Liberty Drive
Bloomington, IN 47403
www.balboapress.com
844-682-1282

Because of the dynamic nature of the Internet, any web addresses or links contained in this book may have changed since publication and may no longer be valid. The views expressed in this work are solely those of the author and do not necessarily reflect the views of the publisher, and the publisher hereby disclaims any responsibility for them.

The author of this book does not dispense medical advice or prescribe the use of any technique as a form of treatment for physical, emotional, or medical problems without the advice of a physician, either directly or indirectly. The intent of the author is only to offer information of a general nature to help you in your quest for emotional and spiritual well-being. In the event you use any of the information in this book for yourself, which is your constitutional right, the author and the publisher assume no responsibility for your actions.

Any people depicted in stock imagery provided by Getty Images are models, and such images are being used for illustrative purposes only. Certain stock imagery © Getty Images.

Cover Design – Saint Tone Productions
Painting of Mary Magdalen by Kim Cintio

MaryMuntoldTRUEstory@gmail.com
Indivinetime.com

Print information available on the last page.

ISBN: 978-1-9822-7063-6 (sc)
ISBN: 978-1-9822-7064-3 (e)

Balboa Press rev. date: 09/24/2021

I dedicate this book and these teachings to every beautiful soul who has crossed my path. You have shared your message to me directly and indirectly. In turn, you gave me the drive to move forward on my journey to share the light.

To my mother, Sandra, for all your love and support throughout the years. Thank you for believing in me to make this all possible. My mom passed away prior to the completion of the book. She now watches over me and will see it all from a higher perspective.

I love you, Mom!

❧ Contents ❧

Acknowledgments

I am extremely grateful to have this opportunity to share Mary's untold *true* story of her life *in her own words.* The bond we share is indescribable. Since learning that she shares my physical body, I have felt her every emotion while writing this book and her teachings. For this, I am eternally grateful. It has been my honor to share her untold story.

To my dear brother, Steve, and nephews, Michael and Scott, for your love and support during the process of writing this book.

Janie Boisclair, my special friend. Thank you for your kindness and expertise in helping me to edit and in sharing your knowledge to assist me in the making of this book with Mary's untold story and teachings.

I appreciate you!

✌ Introduction ✍

I have been a psychic medium, known as a trance channel medium, a clairvoyant (psychic clear seeing), clairaudient (psychic clear hearing), claircognizance (psychic clear sense of knowing), clairsentient (psychic clear feeling, empathy), and clairalience (psychic clear smelling) most of my life. I am delighted to share with you the direct channeling I received from Mary Magdalen herself in the hopes that it will enlighten you as to the truths about her life that have *not been told to date.*

Mary asks that you read her story with an open heart and mind to allow her words to infiltrate your being and to allow you to immerse in her truth in *her own words*. You will not find any of this material in any other form of written history or literature of any type including the Bible, gospels, etc.

My spiritual awakening began in 2006. However, this sacred activation brought so much clarity and awareness forward for me to really understand what was coming together for my future endeavors.

In 2016, while on a sacred journey in Sedona, Arizona, I had a miraculous activation take place while I walked the medicine wheel at Amitabha Stupa Peace Park. It was there in the medicine wheel I was spiritually greeted by five sacred elder ancestors of the land. When they approached me, they cleansed me with sage, also known as smudging, as I smelled it. (Burning sage is used to cleanse a person or space of negative energy, unwanted spirits, or stagnated energies. It is an ancient spiritual ritual and a Native American tradition.) They also blessed me speaking in a language that was foreign to me. It sounded like it was in tongues or chanting like. I immediately felt the love and blessing overwhelm me. A sense of greatness was happening. They then asked me to stand in each direction while they continued to cleanse and bless me.

After they finished, I realized that something of great magnitude had just taken place. I went into the middle of the medicine wheel, stood there, looked up at the heavens with my arms outstretched, and expressed my gratitude. It was at that time that one of the women in my group came by and took a picture of me. That night, when I went to sleep, I had a vivid dream. In the dream, I saw myself with my heart wide-open and sharing massive amounts of love to the masses including all humanity, the animal and plant kingdoms, and the world.

As I sit here writing this, I feel such an immense amount of gratitude for this amazing journey I am on. It was from this moment forward that I realized what was coming forward for me.

Through my channeling experiences, I have learned of my closeness to Mary and how she has already influenced my life.

My hope for you is to find and understand not only the truth about her journey from her own words but also how her wisdom has changed your life.

❧ Chapter 1 ❧

Mary Magdalen's Current Sacred Mission

All italicized print is Mary channeled through Kim Cintio.

Since the time I crossed over to the other side, I have discovered so much more about myself and how things really are. I realized that while I lived on the earth plane that everything was just a mere illusion. My sense of sight and feeling has heightened to a degree that I can see things at a much broader perspective now. My role here on the higher planes is to assist other souls to reach new levels of consciousness, to assist them in remembering who they are, and to help them see things from a higher perspective. Many souls I assist have had some type of connection with me in a previous lifetime.

In the early years, while I was training for this great purpose, I always had a strong sense that I was being prepared for something greater. I did not question it at all as I felt it was in my best interest. It was not until later that

I realized my desire for something of great magnitude was going to take place. After going to Egypt and training in the Temple of Isis, I began to understand more of what was expected of me. It was during that time I became a High Priestess Initiate, which I learned was a very high role for that type of teaching. It was there that I learned a lot about life and energy and how to hold energy for a long period of time. I held the energy for Yeshua during his crucifixion, along with his mother and Elizabeth. (Elizabeth was my best friend and Yeshua's half sister.) These teachings also allowed me to do several healings and initiations on others who were following our mission.

You see, my dear children, our mission was all about teaching others in a patriarchal society about unconditional love (Christ consciousness) and how to apply it in your lives. How to see things differently. Going into your heart space and focusing and projecting love from your heart into everything you do in your life. Very similar to what we are teaching and sharing with all of humanity now. This is what is going to shift your perspective in a very loving manner to create a new way of being. There will be no more fear, judgment, hate, or cruelty of any sort. These are all lower-vibrating energies. The "New Earth," new way of life so to speak, will not allow any of that. Everyone will be vibrating at much higher levels, living their lives with more purpose, abundance, prosperity, and happiness. This is the result of this transition that is taking place on your planet right now. This is what Yeshua and I were trying to do two thousand years ago. Society was not ready at that time.

We (the Universe) are making big strides to break down the old paradigms to transition into the New Earth we are creating through all of you who volunteered to incarnate at this time. You see, my dear children, this is such an exciting time right now. All of you have very important roles in this transition, transformation of the creating of our New Earth. All roles and missions are different. We must respect one another. We are here at this time to bring forth the new way of living in unconditional love of Christ consciousness for all and a new way of being.

Note: My Personal Perspective

I loved learning about their mission, and I find my mission about unconditional love to be parallel to Mary. For me, I find that I first go to my internal feelings and then look outwardly to gauge whether I am looking at a situation born of love or something else. I feel that this is an important lesson to teach because this is what is going to shift humanity into a stronger, more loving and vibrational journey.

How will you help humanity to shift into a more loving vibration? Do you feel connected to Mary's perspective on love?

Workbook Questions

❧ Chapter 1 ❧

Mary Magdalen's Current Sacred Mission

1. Are you aware that you have a greater purpose?
   Do you feel you are being prepared for something bigger? Explain in your own words what that might be.

_____

_____

_____

_____

_____

_____

_____

_____

2. What is your mission and purpose?

_____

_____

_____

_____

_____

_____

_____

3. What is your "role" in society? How does this relate to your mission?

_____

_____

_____

_____

_____

_____

_____

4. Have you noticed any shifts or changes in your consciousness on your journey to your life's mission?

_____

_____

_____

_____

_____

_____

5. Are you ready to expand your thoughts to move forward on your spiritual mission?

_____

_____

_____

_____

_____

_____

_____

6. What will it take to do that?

_____

_____

_____

_____

_____

_____

_____

ೞ

❧ Chapter 2 ❧

Mary and Yeshua's Deep Soul Connection

In order to explain my soul connection with Yeshua, I first need you to understand the difference between soul mate and twin flame relationships.

A soul mate *relationship is finding another soul with which you have had previous lifetimes. These souls are in the same soul group which in each lifetime as we incarnate they come in to teach us lessons that have not been learned from previous lifetimes. They could come in as your sister, brother, mother, father, friend, or lover. Whichever it may be, this soul is here for your soul growth. You feel that special connection when you meet or connect. You feel as if you have known them your entire life. You plan this prior to your incarnation. All members of your circle are soul mates. All are here to teach, learn, and grow. Your spirit guides, guardians, and teachers assist you to stay on your path so that these connections can take place. Everyone has a soul group, and each soul plays a different role in each incarnation. We are all here to assist with their lessons not previously learned from prior lifetimes.*

A twin flame *relationship is quite different. Before we incarnate into a new life, we sit down with our spirit guides, guardians, and teachers and write our soul contract. At a precise time and date, it is written that we are going to meet our spiritual divine partners. This divine union is completely orchestrated by the Universe. Now before the two souls can come together, they must be cleared and healed from all past karma and have a great love for themselves. It's about a clean slate, so to speak, living and working on the same sacred divine spiritual mission on the earth plane and in other dimensions on higher planes of existence while sleeping. One's partner represents the sacred divine feminine or sacred divine masculine union, meaning that this soul acts as a mirror reflection of the other, showing each other a different perspective on every situation that arises. It cannot be in an argumentative way but in a higher sense of self to see things completely different from a higher perspective.*

Twin flames also communicate telepathically, empathically, and can see in each other's energy fields clairvoyantly. They can communicate nonverbally and often do, not only by thoughts but verbally communicating in each other's mind. When one feels off or down, the other compensates for the lost or missing feelings. Twin flames also communicate with each other prior to the actual physical connection. Telepathically, clairvoyantly, and empathically with each other's higher self (the part of the soul that is connected directly to the Universe, Source, God, Creator) and spirit self (the part of the soul in the human body).

Only a small percentage of humanity has this divine partnership. A twin flame can be in a physical body or nonphysical on the other side.

There is a story of when Yeshua and I met in Israel for the first time "by the well." It is true I did meet Yeshua by the well. I had visited the well previously, imagining what it would be like prior to our actual meeting. You see, my dear children, Yeshua and I were twin flames and still are on the other planes of existence.

I had visions of Yeshua and had conversations with him prior to the meeting. His higher self is the one you call Lord Sananda. We got acquainted during that time prior to the actual meeting. So we did have a sense that this was all going to take place. We just did not know when it would be. We followed our guidance and intuition. I felt very excited as I knew in my heart this was going to happen, and it was at the exact time I was at the well that he did appear. When our eyes met, it was pure magic. Words cannot even describe the feelings I had when this happened. The love I felt was so intensified. My whole body quivered with excitement. I knew immediately in my heart that he was the one who was going to help me to grow and evolve on my soul's mission.

He was not only connected to me spiritually, but also my love, my partner, and my life. All the visions and messages I had received prior to the meeting were here. I knew deep down he was the one I had been preparing and waiting for.

Our spiritual mission was to begin.

Yeshua and I spent many nights discussing different subject matter to make our relationship stronger. We did not always agree. We listened with love and respect to simply learn from each other. While we were speaking to masses of people on the mound, I felt so empowered knowing he was near. The love and support for one another is incredibly strong.

Note: My Personal Perspective

I first recognized my twin flame experience and then compared the two. How my twin flame came to me first was as his higher self, and he announced himself to me. An additional benefit I have is I can see him clairvoyantly. I can feel his presence when he arrives and communicate with him telepathically, and we can feel each other empathically. (The higher self is the part of the soul that has the direct connection to the Creator, Universe, God with no ego involved, only pure divine love).

After the acquaintance with his higher self, I was introduced to his etheric self. This is the part of the soul that operates in the human body experience consisting of the ego, and karmic lessons. I have the same type of communication with his higher self as I could communicate with both separately. He has also on some occasions performed healing techniques on me when I have back pain, for example. We take care of each other energetically. He has equivalent gifts and abilities and is at the same level of consciousness as I am.

It must be this way so we can step right into our spiritual mission together. I now know that I feel him strongest through our heart chakra. This all happens in the etheric realm before the actual physical meeting takes place. The feeling of love with this man is so intense that I know it is unlike any love I have ever experienced.

(Be aware that not everyone has a twin flame. Do not let that discourage you. It must be written in your soul's contract whether or not you have this divine sacred union with another soul.)

I will share with you that everyone has a soul mate, and this relationship can be enlightening as well. A love relationship with a soul mate can be empowering and intense as well as show you how to learn from one another about the previous lessons that were not healed or handled with ease and grace from previous lifetimes. There is much growth and expansion in one's journey to be experienced with your soul mate. All of us have many soul mates throughout our lifetime to look forward to. Enjoy the experience!

Workbook Questions

∽ Chapter 2 ∾

Mary and Yeshua's Deep Soul Connection

1. Explain in your own words what a soul mate relationship is and what a twin flame relationship is.

_____

_____

_____

_____

_____

_____

_____

_____

2. What are the differences between the two? Please give examples.

_____

_____

_____

_____

_____

_____

3. Have you ever experienced a telepathic, clairvoyant, or empathic relationship with another soul? If you have, please explain in your own words, and compare your experiences to Mary and Yeshua's relationship.

_____

_____

_____

_____

_____

_____

4. What are your feelings about the truth of Mary and Yeshua's relationship? Feel it in your heart and not what was written in the Bible.

_____

_____

_____

_____

_____

5. If Mary were standing in front of you, what would you say to her?

_____

_____

_____

_____

_____

_____

ॐ

∾ Chapter 3 ✑

Mary's Accomplishments on Earth

My dear children of the light, I would like to express and share with you my role and mission with Yeshua while we were on the earth plane. During our lifetime, society was quite different from the way things are now. And what I mean by that is that it was a patriarchal society. Women did not have a position in society; they were homemakers and child bearers and took care of the children. We were allowed to do nothing else. So with this being said, while we were on our mission together in Jerusalem and speaking and sharing the information we were receiving, Yeshua was always the first to speak, and then I would. It was always acceptable when my beloved spoke, but not when I did. I was able to carry on forward with my role in our mission even though I was looked upon with no respect.

I considered myself a strong woman, regardless of what was said of me. I had the drive and felt in my heart to keep moving forward, and that is what I did. My beloved, Yeshua was always at my side and helped guide me and gave me the confidence to truly move forward. I knew deep down that this is what I was prepared for, and this is what I am here to do, whether it was accepted or not.

My role in this mission was to support my beloved and for him, Yeshua, to support me. We would meditate and pray every day. Many times, and most of the time, we had no idea what we were going to speak about. It was when we approached the mound and everyone got settled that the words began to flow. There was no rehearsal. Yeshua began to speak, and all listened very attentively.

Once he finished, I began. Our words just flowed together. I could always feel my beloved's love overcome me. Once I started to speak, any fear or anxiety I was feeling was lifted. This is what I was talking about earlier with the twin flame *connection. The mutual love support is so very strong as I could feel his loving energy all through my entire being, giving me such a sense of pure love traveling through my entire body—such a strong, loving support. It was almost like our souls merged with one another. It takes my breath away just going back to that time and reliving the memory of it.*

During the time of the crucifixion, my heart dropped as I knew what was about to take place. They came and arrested my beloved Yeshua. Mother (Mother Mary) and I were stricken with fear. We tried desperately not to allow these feelings to show to Yeshua as I knew deep in my heart he would feel my uncertainty. He did everything in his power to stay calm. I knew that he was scared.

Even though we prepared ourselves for this dreaded day, it does not matter how much preparation you have. You still feel human emotion. It was extremely difficult for me to witness my beloved being tortured that way. Yeshua and I were communicating telepathically during the ordeal. I assisted him in going to another place and leaving his physical body while this all took place. He did not feel any pain until he came back into his body. Mother and I were coaching him through the whole ordeal. This was all part of the great mission.

After he was taken down off the cross, he was transported to a holding area under Roman rule. It was there that I, Mother, and Elizabeth came in and out and did energy healing and prayers and applied essential oils on him to help him heal. He was still alive when this was taking place as he did return to his body at this point. We then got permission from the Roman guard to take Yeshua from the holding area onto a cart, and we then removed his body to safety.

We arranged through my father and Yeshua's uncle to take a boat to escape. The intention was set to go far away from Israel as from here on out we were fleeing in fear of being found out. We had my beloved Yeshua covered up in the boat along with the rest of the family. We landed on the shore of southern Gaul, which now is southern France, Saintes-Maries-de-la-Mer. It was there we started our new life. My main concern was to find shelter to nurse my beloved back to health. We did as we met a wonderful loving family that took us in until we found a place to call our own. It took several months for my beloved to heal and to come back to himself.

After my beloved was healed, he was not the same man he was. Yes, he was always by my side, and we continued our mission together. However, it was I who was the main speaker to the people as Yeshua was now there for my support. He did, once he was fully recovered, speak on some occasion. For the most part, it was I who was the main speaker of the information coming through. You can say our roles had been reversed.

We did still continue with our spiritual mission on a daily basis. We stayed mostly in caves and were continuously on the run. We had a fear of being found out. If word got out that my beloved had survived the crucifixion, we all would have been killed.

Every time we got the news that the Roman Catholic army was close by, we picked up and fled the area. We did, however, settle in some places for a period of time. One place was Rennes-le-Chateau. A lovely area where the earth was fertile for our vegetables and our children could play freely with no worry. It was located on a mountaintop with deep valleys all around. There were several caves where we would sit and meditate for days. Yeshua felt most comfortable there. He said he could relax and ascend to the higher realms without any fear of being found out. It gave him great comfort, and we did this very often. He was able to gain so much insight during these stays, as did all the Magdalens.

Note: My Personal Perspective

When I look back at my life so far, I feel that I have been able to accomplish the opening of hearts and awareness to others in their own spirituality. I feel that my journey on this earth is to assist others in their own enlightenment as Yeshua and Mary did in their lifetime. I continue to stay on my mission, even though I feel that I am often misunderstood as to my mission's purpose. I, like Mary, also consider myself a strong woman, and I rarely let the opinion of the outside world derail me.

What resonates with you as to your role on this earth?

Workbook Questions

❧ Chapter 3 ❧

Mary's Accomplishments on Earth

1. Do you feel you have the same drive as Mary did? If so, please explain.

_____

_____

_____

_____

_____

_____

_____

_____

2. Do you question your guidance? Mary mentioned she felt the need to push through all obstacles. Do you feel you have that same drive to accomplish what is expected of you at any given time? If so, just know you are in alignment of the divine plan that is written in your soul's contract. You are on the right path. (Your soul contract is written by you with your spirit guide's assistance prior to your incarnation in this lifetime.)

_____

_____

_____

_____

_____

_____

_____

_____

_____

_____

3. How do you feel you can apply what you were prepared for in your divine plan, your role, your mission?

   Sharing what you are feeling is letting the Universe know you are serious about what is expected of you. When you share, they will bring you more.

   _____

   _____

   _____

   _____

   _____

   _____

4. How does your life compare to Mary's life?

   _____

   _____

   _____

   _____

   _____

5. What is similar, and what is different?

_____

_____

_____

_____

_____

_____

_____

ૐ

❧ Chapter 4 ❧

Knights Templar and Their Importance to Mary

The Knights Templar were an organization of men who defended my honor and protected Yeshua and me and all of the Magdalens. Like military police. They were also very disciplined in their ways. They were highly respected and basically had control of the land a large portion of the time. They were the elite ones known as the architects, the bankers, and the businessmen who built and developed an empire, so to speak. They are responsible for building many of the castles and places of worship all over Israel, Portugal, Italy, Spain, the United Kingdom and other parts of Europe as well as Brazil. Many were and had family members who were Cathars. (I will explain and speak about the Cathars in module 3.) Their organization continued and became stronger in time. They continued their legacy hundreds of years after my lifetime.

The Templars lived according to certain codes and lineages, very similar to the practices Yeshua and I spoke about in our teachings. This is very different from what is written in your Bible. As mentioned in module 1, many of the quotes, sayings, and teachings mentioned in the Bible were not the true word we spoke of in our gatherings. The Bible was an interpretation of our gatherings.

The Templars lived by a code of honor and respect. They made it their life practice to live up to their code of ethics. They also kept everything confidential to protect themselves from the fears of the Catholic Church. The Catholic Church and the Roman army, which worked with the church, did not like the fact that many followed their direction. As a form of control, the church had all the Templars killed and exterminated as they did with any group that did not follow their beliefs at that time. The church wanted full control of their beliefs. Presently, there are secret groups who carry the same ethics and practices of the Templars.

Note: My Personal Perspective

Through my own traveling experiences, the information I learned about the Templars piqued my interest. Through my channeling of Mary in this book, I was filled in on all the details that I was unaware of. With that being said, I am highly interested to learn more about Mary's life and how she came to be the amazing humanitarian that she was and still is.

As I mentioned before, I am thirsty to learn more about the Knights Templars and the Cathars. (See module 3 to learn more about the Cathars.) During my travels all over Europe and the United Kingdom, I visited many castles and churches that were built by the Knights Templar. I am always so fascinated by these amazing gothic structures that include prophets and mystics carved in stone with perfection. It makes you think about how back then they did not have very many tools to work with like the present day. I would stand in amazement with the detail of the carvings.

Inside the churches were also many clues of Mary and Yeshua's life and how much was actually hidden from humanity. I found that to be so interesting. I look forward to visiting Brazil, Portugal, and other places where the Templars thrived.

Workbook Questions

❧ Chapter 4 ❧

Knights Templar and Their Importance to Mary

1. Do you feel confident and protected when speaking your truth? Are you aware and discerning when speaking to others about your spiritual direction?

_____

_____

_____

_____

_____

_____

_____

2. Do you feel comfortable and confident with the information you share?

_____

_____

_____

_____

_____

_____

_____

3. Are you selective with the people you surround yourself with? It is very important to surround yourself with other like-minded people who respect you and support your opinion.

_____

_____

_____

_____

_____

_____

4. Do you feel you have a lot to offer others with your open heart?

_____

_____

_____

_____

_____

_____

5. Explain what it feels like to have or desire to have a loyal and respectful tribe who supports and loves you.

_____

_____

_____

_____

_____

_____

૭

Congratulations!

You have just completed module 2. To learn about Mary's untold *true* story and teachings, see the other modules that are available.

Module 1 - My Introduction to Mary Magdalen and How She Came into My Awareness
Module 3 - Mary Magdalen's Relationship with Archangel Michael
Module 4 - Nontruths Told about Mary Magdalen

Learn more, shared in detail, in the book titled *The Untold True Story of Mary Magdalen in Her Own Words.*

Printed in the United States
by Baker & Taylor Publisher Services

Printed in the United States
by Baker & Taylor Publisher Services